INQUISITION

ALSO BY
KAZIM ALI

POETRY

All One's Blue: New and Selected Poems (HarperCollins India)

Sky Ward (Wesleyan University Press)

The Far Mosque (Alice James)

The Fortieth Day (BOA Editions)

CROSS GENRE

Bright Felon: Autobiography and Cities (Wesleyan University Press)

Wind Instrument (Spork Press)

NONFICTION

Orange Alert: Essays on Poetry, Art, and the Architecture of Silence (University of Michigan Press)

Fasting for Ramadan (Tupelo Press)

Resident Alien: On Border-crossing and the Undocumented Divine (University of Michigan Press)

Anaïs Nin: An Unprofessional Study (Agape Editions)

Silver Road: Essays, Maps & Calligraphies (Tupelo Press)

FICTION

Quinn's Passage (blazeVox books)

The Disappearance of Seth (Etruscan Press)

Uncle Sharif's Life in Music (Sibling Rivalry Press)

The Secret Room: A String Quartet (Kaya Press)

TRANSLATION

Water's Footfall by Sohrab Sepehri (Omnidawn Press)

Oasis of Now: Selected Poems by Sohrab Sepehri (BOA Editions)

When the Night Agrees to Speak to Me by Ananda Devi (HarperCollins India)

L'amour by Marguerite Duras (Open Letter Books)

Abahn Sabana David by Marguerite Duras (Open Letter Books)

KAZIM ALI

INQUISITION

WESLEYAN UNIVERSITY PRESS

MIDDLETOWN, CONNECTICUT

Wesleyan University Press
Middletown CT 06459
www.wesleyan.edu/wespress
2018 © Mohammad Kazim Ali
Manufactured in the United States of America
Designed and typeset in Fresco by Eric M. Brooks

Library of Congress Cataloging-in-Publication Data
NAMES: Ali, Kazim, 1971-, author
TITLE: Inquisition / Kazim Ali
DESCRIPTION: Middletown, Connecticut : Wesleyan University
    Press, [2018] | Series: Wesleyan Poetry
IDENTIFIERS: LCCN 2017018699 (print) |
    LCCN 2017023492 (ebook) | ISBN 9780819577719 (ebook) |
    ISBN 9780819577702 (cloth: alk. paper) |
    ISBN 9780819577627 (pbk.: alk. paper)
CLASSIFICATION: LCC PS3601.L375 (ebook) |
    LCC PS3601.L375 A6 2018 (print) | DDC 811/.6—dc23
LC record available at https://lccn.loc.gov/2017018699

5 4 3 2 1

ART WORKS.
arts.gov

*This project is supported in part by an award
from the National Endowment for the Arts*

CONTENTS

May 1

I

The Earthquake Days 5

Flower Gate 8

The Astronomer 9

Abu Nuwas 11

Light House 12

John 14

Night: A Celan Variation 15

Phenomenal Survivals of Death in the Mountains 17

Atlas 19

His Mosaic Prayer 20

System Error 21

Sent Mail 22

Origin Story 23

Saraswati Puja 26

The Failure of Navigation in the Valley 28

II

Trick 33

Messy Drunk 34

Letter to Zephyr from the Once-Boy Hyacinth 35

The Labors of Psyche 36

Letter to Hyacinth from the Once-Wind Zephyr 38

Persephone as a Boy 39

Drone 40

Chopping the Birch 41

The Tornado 43

Screen Door 44

Checkpoint 45

The Dress-Maker of Galilee 46

Sacrifice 47

Amerika the Beautiful 50

Inquisition 54

III

Bird Hospital 59

Marie's Crisis 60

Missal 63

Yannis Ritsos 64

Random Search 66

Square 67

Sun Ward 68

Text Cloud Anthology 70

Forgotten Equations 72

The Astronomer's Son 74

All One's Blue 76

Door Between You 77

Son of History 78

Legislature 79

Apasmara Climbs to the Mountain Lake 83

Acknowledgments 87

Notes 89

INQUISITION

MAY

And so it came my last day in the sunset, fog sluicing over me.

I turn east in the gaunt dawn and sue the blue dizzy.

At least in the unloving years I had my difference to wield.

THE EARTHQUAKE DAYS

In the earthquake days I could not hear you over the din or it might have been
the dinner bell but that's odd
because I'm usually the one
cooking up if not dinner then
a plan to build new fault lines through the dangerous valley

I can't give you an answer right now because I'm late for my resurrection,
the one where I step into my angel offices and fuck
the sun delirious.
That eclipse last week? Because of me
You're welcome

The postman rattles up with your counteroffer and I'm off
to a yoga class avoiding your call yes like the plague
because son you can read
in the dark and I have no
hiding place left

We walk hand in hand down the hill
into the Castro
avoiding the nudist protest not because we are afraid but
because we already know all about this city, its engineered foundations,
its earthquake-proofed buildings, the sea walls

No tempest will catch us unaware
while we claim our share of
the province of penumbral affections —
You have no reason
to trust me but I swear I lie

down in this metal box as it thunders and looks
inside my brain. I am terrified nothing
is wrong because otherwise
how will I rewrite the maps unmoored
a deep sea a moor a cosmonaut

Who needs saving more
than the one who forgot
how the lazy cartographer mislabeled
his birthplace as Loss?
Riding the bus out to the end of the lines and back

I collect trash for art, oil spill, spent forest, the mind
is at work and everything is at stake — I demand
statehood for my states of mind, senators
for my failure, my disappointment, the slander
and my brain unmapped reveals no

explanation for danger the ground untamed
I make paintings of nothing and
stand before them like mirrors
I only recently became a man but I do
not want to let go of my boy-weakness

instead I want to meet God in heaven and in long psychotropic odes
have Him send me again digging in the dirt to unleash
tantric animal governors to lay down
the orgasmic law twice skewered and miserable
in the old photographs, miserable in my body, huddled

next to my mother, recently permed and aglow so unaware
of what is about to hit her — that I am the answer to Bhanu's question:
"Who is responsible for the suffering of your mother?" and so sick
I considered that sickness
could bring us closer and Shahid and Allen in heaven

shake me by the shoulders three times because they want me
to know that this world is worth its
trembling. At the next table over a mother
tries to reconcile her bickering sons
I have no brother but the one

I invent has always got my back, he drowns
out the mullahs so my mother can finally hear me
In a different book Jesus
never suffered, never was flogged or died
went whole into heaven without passion

Shall I then deny myself passport through the stark places
unsalvageable, imagine it, the Mother
of Sorrows did never grieve in the new season
trees smell of semen and the tectonic plates
make their latest explosive move:

to transubstantiate my claim
by unraveling this city down to stone
Everyone I know wants to douse
the fire, flee the endless aftershocks,
untangle every vexing question

You owe me this witness

I owe you flames

FLOWER GATE

Edged in petals I affix myself to the gate
at every appointed prayer hour

Seed pods scatter in silver dusk
Green cypresses minaret the sky

My disobedient body aspires and I
when music pierces inland hand in hand

devour this arbor of forgetting
and take one last shot at sharing your fiery fate

In the end I am not you
Not a garden nor a gate

But just a scruffy hustler, willing to hop the fence
and spend himself bare to nothing

THE ASTRONOMER

Adamant in his argument against winter he plots the distance
to the horizon by graphing the shape of a tree against its green,
calculating the sum of the wind when yesterday is taken from it.

His azimuth splendor maps the city twice in time
and he feels the drag of the tide pulling him along through millennia
into other cities each of which existed here in this same place.

Afternoon in sunlight, he climbs up the mountain
and arrives at the flower-gate leading to the garden on the slope,
there being no more resistant surface

upon which eternity could make its useless claim:
that the prayers he learned
all his life mean no more to him.

Thrust up from the dark of the earth only to wither,
how are flowers in any way supposed to understand god?
They are no better than a human body that seeds and sprouts and dies.

And even if a body were to remake itself or rename itself as different matter
what would it matter? Briefly he wonders: is he a river then,
furiously plotting a course? Or the boat floating down it or the person inside?

No mathematics can plot the path from a body that doesn't exist to a city
that doesn't exist. The storm won't abate, its numbers irrational, tempers extreme,
like that of another poet-mathematician who lived a thousand years back or maybe

one who lived a thousand years on, drawing patterns in stone to cut for tiles,
piecing together a map of the universe: seven small planets swinging
their cosmography of charlatan destinies. Is that his future or history unmapped?

He remembers that the sage Ali warned the astrologers to cease telling fortunes
not on account of potential infidelity but because the book of the stars
was impossibly infinite and so many bodies yet unseen and uncharted

that any divination risked planetary imbalance. And so he never knew
which of the unknown constellations truly governed his kismet:
Fairy Prince. Lonely Brother. Angry Son.

At any rate, stubborn as a volunteer, he appears in the flower beds.
Annually he clamors to be, along with the hyacinths, tulips and orchids,
gathered and carried to portal adornment.

He broke his way through the glittering dome by guts and calculus,
that science meant to plot the relationship between different objects
unspeakable that move through the cosmos at varying speeds.

In the kingdom of heaven the belt of Orion is no belt at all
but stars separated by galaxies and light-centuries.
His hands on the bars of the garden gate grow dark in the dimming light.

And suddenly he understands the horizon is not the end of the world
but like god and the unfound planets it is only the end of his knowing
about the world, like that call to prayer unspooling its rebuke

over silver-leafed olives and cypresses
on the way down to make an unresting vow
to the blue devastation of the unbound sea.

ABU NUWAS

to Marilyn Hacker

Halfway between the northern and southern sky

Hangs the constellation of Abu Nuwas

Who drunk and in love knelt at places rivers split

To refuse all paths and offer his mosaic prayer

Unhinged he peeled from yellow-leafed birches enough paper

To fashion a barque and make for the moon

Floating in the moment where one wave becomes another

Amber driftwood or beach glass or lost unmapped stars reciting

We are what produces itself sanded and cast adrift

Precisely at the horizon and so eternally unseen

One note emerges from the drizzle of sound

What finally somehow though endless does wash ashore

LIGHT HOUSE

When we spoke submerged
That smooth wheel of sound
Some nonsense did echo
A rescue clarion

Siren in scarlet teeming
I reach into you ashore
Everything hull quivers
My name I don't know

To prove unspasmed loyalty
I from shipwreck swam
With only these clothes on my back
Begged anchorless through the town

For one who knows the way
A body floats in death
Salt drunk I stumbled
Swaying down the path

I never-know the way to you
For "a grid is halfway between"
Hidden and returning
"a rectangular system and a veil"

Someone I never yet knew
Haunts me through the streets
"Technique is hazard"
to lonely evangelists

Opon night resound the impossible
Empty cello case or drunk text
Then every form happens
An anarchy of sense

Salt and air your name
Body's borders quiver
Always still a gale
Scattering intention

Whose inside voice recruits
A scribe to grind a lens
Where could silence sound a note
to its incandescence spend

JOHN

Who was I when I was writing this name

Copper oxidizes to green

Air packs itself tight in the seed

Seed unspools in the ground writing the biography of dirt

A little down the road another tower is going up

A man holds his briefcase over his head like an umbrella

In the rain bodies are soft and disappear into sound

On John Street almost choking on loneliness

And the waters of the river nothing so much as the air around us and ash

What would outlive us drifts sparkling into the October air

When you ask who am I past this storm-tossed vessel

The one you're always bailing out

It is just another way to ignore this constant unraveling

This always reaching for an end when clearly there's no end in sight

NIGHT: A CELAN VARIATION

to David Young

1

Rockward rubble. Violin that slices through
Time's wound

Look then at the limit
Clock runs down
You stay the same
Daphne-like I ditch you

For nothing but an always-reaching

2

Rock word rumble. Rumble the earth that thunders
A drum a sound the stand-alone landscape

Deep inside I
As in the earth do move
Frozen in the frame
Picture of my youthful smile

Light writes me down to the bone

3

Landslide
Nothing but sound
No letter to tell anyone I'm safe

I'm in it
Beneath the surface of the earth waiting
Days without rescue
I wed the stone

4

What's left over. A broken sound that offers
A flickering piece to limn

The look that passes between us
Out of time
Fix you in time
I could hold you
But would it
Last

5

Earth comes after. Sound of a vessel breaking
And what's inside pours out

Seeds have a mission too
Cast an eye over the landscape
You think what changes doesn't change
Human body in the earth
Tree growing over it

That's how it goes

PHENOMENAL SURVIVALS OF DEATH IN THE MOUNTAINS

after Louise Glück

1

Jacketed by mountains does the self of sulfur
Send itself to rock or vapor
Cleft do You breathe my surface
Beneath or above the earth's surface
When in the valley I trafficked in sound
I dreamt of a man his hands bound
By shafts of sun and cloud
Saying, "I am Saint Everyone.
In my pocket a spool of piano wire."
Awake in the predawn
I will fill this coffin of stone

2

Awake I unchime
Tickets to heaven all validated, declined
On the third night thrust
The monsoon, my Saint Everyone lust
Played out and the cloud-craft
Unloosed from the rock pier, reft
By thunder. Abandoned by death
And sun I wild and stunned
Wandered the unmarked road
Where my bones still lie in the earth
Amid yarrow and madder and woad

3

If you press your ear to solid stone
Will you hear the body's hard equation
Turn solvent as it quivers
Monsoon a doorway to forever
Took oars away and promised
Saint Everyone carried only orchids
You are not buried, have no money
Body hold fire, hold water and loam
Practice early primal tunes
Night long fled but aloft unseen
Pierced I am by moon-stunned noon

4

Acres of sky condense to cobalt blue
In my pocket tides of dirt spill new
Outward I am borne
To myself sworn and inside worn

From this shore I windward grow
And thorny border cross
My first body built sturdy from loss
My second from spans of cloud and snow

ATLAS

Fossil mortar me
Holding the world up with my breath
Its shoulders seem

Wood to dust
Body of time spilling must
I again be born as ravine

Or revenant I am ravenous to remain
No world wheels raining
To spy on god thunder

Spring I unravel down and now
How the earth lifts up off me
How lightly lies what I think I know

HIS MOSAIC PRAYER

Trial by magnolia
You never understand

Sane and unchanged
Strip down to rain

Cross examined by
Northern lights

My wont was to know you
Uncovered cup of sulfured sun

Struck my bell of breath
Unreachable this ruin of effort

Muttered perfumed profanity
Unsolvable these equations

Unanswerable these letters
Of despair this air that errs

SYSTEM ERROR

Quiver thin
Ash wind

Sudden tear
Hold you in

Season turn
Ash and I

Unbelieve
Tempest limb

Lidless vessel
Errant sin

To the self
No system

SENT MAIL

Lost in your outbox collecting dust are all the messages
you wanted to send to Night the silent whisperer asking
over and over "brother do you believe in god"

I sent the river and now lie down for the part where you split me
from the banks one silver minute before vision when Death
crashes every system and you emigrate to the city that isn't on any maps

The roads which once led there have forests planted across them
and still burning beneath the surface I believe even now in the body
as a spiritual solution believe that maps in error still lead somewhere

I wait for your answer our chat window still open huddling in the dark
because some drunk late-night hooligan is banging at the door insisting
he's you says he's come back he still lives here he won't take no for an answer

ORIGIN STORY

Someone always asks me "where are you from"
And I want to say a body is a body of matter flung
From all corners of the universe and I am a patriot
Of breath of sin of the endless clamor out the window
But what I say is I am from nowhere
Which is also a convenience a kind of lie

When I was sitting in the Mumbai airport this January
On a forty-hour layover rushing home because
My mother had had a stroke and was not yet verbal
I wondered about my words
Perhaps I am from my words
Because the basic biography is ordinary

Born in Croydon to a mother and a father who
On different sides of a national border
Were married in wartime and had to reunite in England
The only place they could both get to
Born at home — 76 Bingham Street
Midwived and not doctored into the world

Taken back to India when the war was over
Where I came into language and of the seven
That were spoken in the house I began speaking four as the same
Then to the cold Canadian north we went to a town that no longer exists
On the other side of Cross Lake from the Indians
Who lost everything because of the dam my father was helping to build

Then to Winnipeg then to New York City
Then to Buffalo
Which I can claim
I can say I am from Buffalo because
It is a city of poets
The city of Lucille Clifton

I arrive there in cold January to find my mother
A little slowed down but still self-possessed enough
To cook meals for everyone
Even if she didn't remember the names for all the spices she was using
She talks by the time I arrive but slowly and deliberately
And she has to listen very carefully to be able to respond

She pauses while she talks and cocks her head while she thinks
She does not criticize me nor say anything about my wild hair
Our ordinary silence does not seem as suffocating
Because I wait patiently while she strains to find each word
And what on earth does it mean that
I almost like my mother better this way

When she goes to her medical appointment
I get out my copy of *good woman* and comb through its lines
To find the addresses where Lucille Clifton grew up and lived
I climb into the car with a map and a journal and drive
Through the snow to find those places and take photographs
Of the empty lots where the houses once stood

Listen:
I have no answer to your question
I am not kidding when I tell you:

I earned my own voice
The shape it makes in the world holds me
I have no hometown no mother tongue

I have not been a good son

SARASWATI PUJA

1

On the train we knew neither when we would arrive nor the name of any station along the fog-laden way.

The taxi driver lied about our hotel being full, stopping in a dark alley.

I insisted we drive on but the way was blocked by the raving Saraswati Puja.

A street full of men, stripped to the waist, dancing like houses on fire, heading down to the river.

One took my hand and pulled me to him but we pressed on through the rickshaw-mounted speakers, bass lines of the strobe-sworn mantras thumping.

Our hotel clerk claimed it really was full so the taxi driver found us another.

You leaned out the window of the room, snapping photos of the puja-rave.

I huddled on the bed, the racket of the train on the tracks still hiving in my ear.

2

On the water in the morning dark shapes emerge

Sewn on the surface of god and ardor:

History a hysterical marigold bloom,

Oarsman pulling with beautiful rhythm,

his eyes covered by dark glasses

Dismembered reed arms float past, Saraswati comes apart

His oar dips in, crushing the floating marigolds

At the Jain ghat a huge painted swastika,

symbol unmoored from meaning

I want him to take off his glasses, to look at me

Open his orange lips, flower-stained and speak to me

What do we have to do to own our life

Water has no architecture in warm places

It will not stay where it is spilled

THE FAILURE OF NAVIGATION IN THE VALLEY   *to C.D. Wright*

No body is fixed in position no one can be known

Still I am read by satellites my tendencies extrapolated

In the mountains I have no GPS I don't know where to go

There are those trees their leaves flicker like little jewels a whole bucketful

Darkness stares back are you even human anymore

I close the curtains at night not because I think others will see in

Turn left there but so I do not see the reflection that is pure dark

I am not afraid of anything oh is that so

Citizen bear do this place not belong to you

Unseen I wander through the thorny place of what I no that ain't it

No fear can be knew can be none fuck how do you spell it

I held a heavy jade pendant in my hand once not in this valley in another

In the range of limited human experience how many places are there really

I don't even have to look at the earth anymore I just have to listen

Now that hillbilly whisper guides me which way to turn how far up the turn is

Drawling like moonshine we're really off the grid now

Making wild prayers to the green dark which kind do you mean

What moonshine grid prayers or dark does it matter it matters

Thank god we thought of having her record this voice every kind

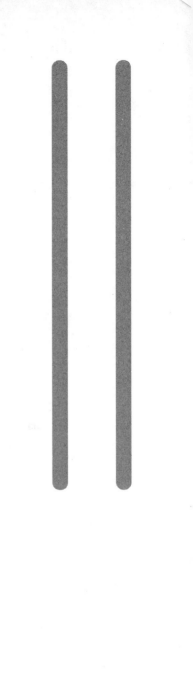

TRICK

Your life among cinematic disasters: tidal wave, swamp thing, tsunami

A wickedly souped-up bore just minutes before the lights go on

Doubly pathetic because daylight savings offered you an extra empty hour

You count your body up in coins and curses and think:

There must be another body inside me, tougher, sunnier, more beautiful

If only I could fuck him free

And the one you want, the dirty blond with the filthy mouth
and pierced tongue is long gone and you are what you've always been:

A squirrelly punk, dizzy with gin, losing your shirt, climbing into the cage

MESSY DRUNK

Dizzy he lifts himself unhitched from this shape hovering at the bar
Streams outside into the alley sparkling with green glass and asphalt

Mixed in an ocean of blue paint spreads himself thin on every surface
His body decants onto the sticky ground

Inside again a ubiquitous charmer tricking the DJ into buying his next round
He is on a mission to see the crack of the sun filter through the dark windows

Day could peel the scab of night away
Though regurgitated to emptiness still he dry heaves

Spun then in a dozen different directions at once
Wakes up on the other side of town, on the roof of a building he doesn't know

Keys to my place forgotten on some table do you know who I am what my name is
From three in the morning I woke myself south driving for the bridge

The wheel spinning under my hands at the second light I go left I haven't eaten
My senselessness unsaid prayers condensing in my mouth

This morning at five I started across the bridge on foot I forgot where I parked
Will I find the lost key left somewhere between the club and the roof

In my mind I was holding it but now I think I never had it that it's still at home
Good because it's not lost bad because I'm locked out

I don't want to be lost anymore to pray only for the dead
Return me to the kingdom where I learned to traffic in muscles and lust

Who am I where is my home who will be there to let me in

LETTER TO ZEPHYR FROM THE ONCE-BOY HYACINTH

Unhook each point from the silver-backed sky.
Unfasten the buttons of my winter jacket and petal me.

Dear fickle once-a-year wonder, reach for me even now, will you,
but know my stem wanders lightward even as your gusts thrust
through the soil into me. Rage in your comely way but know
you arrived each year on his heels, that yellow timeless fire-starter
who shone madly on me even in the cold months. Perhaps I lack
vision, lying with the wonder that arrived first but I thought only
to master my mother's ken. Take comfort at least that I know
it was your roughness that invented me, made beautiful my ruin.

More than merely warm me, you murdered me into music.
You killed my fearful youth and brought me to flower.

THE LABORS OF PSYCHE

Sail or spin I endless ember

In the house of flowers am undone

My crime comes in hot slicks

Plunder now each crushed night

Skylight open wide to snow

Very coldly thrust through

Look now at each unmapped surface

Very hungry spun smooth

Who in the dark comes to pounce

Drinking heat straight from the bottle

My mouth deeply tongued and

By swollen bud's dehiscence opened

You lie on top of me in this siren cave

Breathing whirl of duende innuendo

Come now together between anarchy and will

Bright pharo of flower throat

My fortune lines do still bewilder

Eternal spring now pistil thin

You spin me psychophonic to corolla harbor

Nocturne thrust you exhale I sunder

LETTER TO HYACINTH FROM THE ONCE-WIND ZEPHYR

It should be a letter
To the man inside
I could not become

Dressed in yellow and green
the colors of spring
So I could leave death

In its chamber veined
With deep ore
I've no more to tell you

Last winter I climbed
The mountains of Musoorie
To hear frozen peals of bell and wire

A silver thread of sound
Sky to navel
Drew me

like the black strip
in a flower's throat
meant to guide you in

I lie now in winter
Dormant and mordant
and I cereus bloom

PERSEPHONE AS A BOY

His father used to say, "Your face is like a flower."

At seven each morning he wakes with the sun, imagines it burning
through the window. He dreams he has cancer burning through his skin
but has never been to a doctor.

Yesterday he imagined a death even better, spectacular and violent: crazy
taxi, stray bullet, runaway train—

In the final scene of this film he's lying there with wide eyes,
mouth trembling, struggling to speak to his father,

who is for some reason in New York with him,
holding his hand and saying his scripted lines,
"Don't try to say anything. I love you."

At seven-forty-five he throws back the covers, puts a jacket on over his
pajamas and walks to the corner store for small things he doesn't need,
just to remind himself he is alive: daisies, pomegranates, green tea, salt.

Passing the subway stairs on his way home he realizes he could go
underground here and, by ticket and transfer, not emerge again from the
earth for hundreds of miles.

DRONE

Do strangers make you human

Science fiction visiting bodies as cold fact

What unknown numbers govern our genes or phones

A constant thrum from outer space

Snow makes a sound in sand

You are seen from far above

Will the myth explain you

Unheard and vanished

Bodies dismember to dirt

Hardly alive, hardly a person anymore

Who will I be next and in that life will you know me

CHOPPING THE BIRCH

With an ax I hack at the birch's hard trunk and fold paper boats in the mouth of day.

I wonder what opens inside wild this unyielding trunk.

Condemned to this chore, convinced it is holy but thinking only of the paparazzi of fireflies ablaze in the yard.

I had just returned from Mumbai where on the last day delirious with heat I made my way across the causeway to the Haji Ali Dargah to hear the qawali singers.

Am I even in the world? I wondered.

The story goes that Haji Ali left for pilgrimage but on the way his ship was wrecked in the storm and his body lost at sea.

When did I climb into this body touched and made by a hundred people who daily also climb inside.

The paparazzi chase me indoors. Like God they want only to see me, like God I want only to be seen.

As for Haji Ali, his body washed ashore of all places in the world at the exact point he initially embarked.

The tree will not be chopped, its paper it will not yield.

Three times me equals what. Why if God and I want the same thing are we having such a hard time making this relationship work?

Even if it's true that we choose our own chains, how when you are expelled from the garden are you supposed to still sing to Him that did it to you?

THE TORNADO

The tornado has not yet blown through the window,
scattering spoons, shattering the cups and glasses,
has not yet thrown the room sideways
through the back door.

I am left, abandoned at the supper table
agreeing then to be reborn. Cutlery clatters
up into a dangerous necklace, and part of me yearns
to flee, not down to safety but out into the fields.

If I hadn't prayed for wind would the ocean of air
ever have dropped down toward me and come?
Out of the corner of my eye the car suspended eight feet
above the ground, the rain streaming so briefly upward.

All I want is to love forever, for the door to open,
the family to return, for the meal to be served,
but as forks and knives swirl up from garland
to halo, the weeping house agrees to fall down.

SCREEN DOOR

Banging
in the wind

Impossible
adornment

Sun strummed
I am played

and continue
to explain to air

my language
of screen and ore

improvised
over centuries

the kind of door
I always wanted

to be: closed
but open

CHECKPOINT

"I do not know" is stamped indelibly on my passport so I am marked always for further interrogation.

Adam, the first man, asks me again and again "What are you doing in our country?"

I tell him, "My intention was to go to the place called the Hill of Spring and paint my nails gold."

Risen again from the ocean floor the rocks declare a state of emergency.

Then Eve comes, then other women, then other men, all asking me the same question as if my answer would change so each time I try to change it.

"I have come to dress myself in the salt of the sunken sea."

"I came to write my name down in the peals of bells sealed in a crease of the still fallen wall."

"I will go to the outskirts of the place called the Hill of God and pick carob pods and sumac and practice yoga."

Adam's army has learned twenty-six different words for "no."

Wild fires leap from tree to tree, an arboreal *intifada*.

Water shrinks back from its table in shame.

THE DRESS-MAKER OF GALILEE

He wears himself down wild uncertain,
laps the frayed thread-end
with his clumsy tongue.

He wants to know as well what the body
and its coverings could teach him about
genders of flesh.

The Druze have a secret book.
Some know what's in it,
some don't. No one minds.

His voice falls to pieces when he claims
for himself the spaces
of flowers or silk.

At the worried seam of the border between
what is taught and what is felt, some Druze know
we are all about to switch genders.

With eyes the same silver as his tailor's needle,
in the globe of barbarous heat
he stakes his claim stitch by stich.

He never learned how to behave.
He knows only he must sew one piece to another
and spike heaven sense

SACRIFICE

In the spring after it warmed and cooled again we ran out before sunset to wrap the peach tree,
eleven budded branches worth saving if we could only find the time

The apples, the pears, even the plums, are blissfully ignorant of the danger one cold night poses to the peach,
just as the two brothers, never in the story at the same time, have no idea fate has held them fast

Eleven stars in the sky Jacob saw to warn him of the jealousy of brothers for a brother
and though we wrapped and wrapped the tree we couldn't tell if our labors were in time

Ishmael's is the story of *samood*: upon hearing the horrifying chore his father has been set to by God
he says "father, do what you have been commanded to do. You will find me among the steadfast."

That word, *samood*, is said to define the Palestinian spirit,
though there are those who translate it not as "steadfast" but as "stubborn" in this time

Isaac's story is shock at what God is capable of asking: "But father," the boy asks
upon arrival at the thicket, "Where is the ram?" thinking it escaped from its bonds, was too fast

The stubborn peach tree that lasted all winter will not listen to the climate-changed spring
or the stubborn son who still awaits his father's phone call at bedtime

I know something about going by different names and even switching bodies since my body too is said by some
to be against god. But how can what God utters fit into human ears, His languages are never learned fast

It is that word Ishmael utters to his father when Abraham recounts his dream, *samood*,
and isn't that what every patient farmer wants — a tree that will bear sweet fruit in its mature time

So when you undertake the sacrifice are you commemorating your ability as a human to question God
or are you celebrating the faith you have in your own body even if time moves too fast?

Isaac and Ishmael were more than reluctant brothers, they may well have been
the same son since their chronology in the different mythologies unravels in time

And for what purpose do you then draw the knife across the throat of another?
Might the ram too deserve haven and from the killing you could fast?

Our trees lie in a ring, dependent on one another for warmth but also for pollination
and who can say that one tree is not another moving through time

Enough! for the peach tree the time to bloom has not come but it has already happened,
all we can hope is to protect it for the night and pray morning comes fast

Says one story Ishmael was the first son, son of a first wife, and that the other brother also became
the father of prophets but was not him, the chosen one taken up to the thicket that time

when even the bodies of children can be undressed down to their guts and bones. What will you not be willing to do in the name of the God-given, in wartime?

We have no prayer left for the trees or children. Trees are uprooted and the homes of the children are demolished, abandoned are the olive groves and bullet-ridden are fields of wild thyme.

And what is it that you unbibled but not released are supposed to do when your small god-sized father asks you to come. He looks at you with love but has a knife in his hand. Decide fast.

The walls shake, the roof is tapped and you do not have an eternity but thirty seconds to survey the room and leave behind the life you have known. What will you take with you? Choose. *Quick.* Out of time —

AMERIKA THE BEAUTIFUL

after "Bush's War" by Robert Hass

I open into a space of unknowing flickers
but frightened by the evidence and unwilling
to release an old and instinctual clench
in my gut. I open a new document and type
"Trump's America" to see if that will make
reality more real, help me to see into the future. What if
I recounted something ordinary, some old story
that had nothing to do with gold star mothers shamed
or my cousins and uncles forced to register
because of their faith. Hyderabad is a southern city
though it doesn't feel like one on account of its
Urdu heritage, and situated right on top
of what used to be a mountain range seventy or eighty
million years ago. To the east the hills ruckle gently
the subcontinent on their way to the Bay of Bengal
and to the south and west the boulders break
and break and shatter into the parched plains. Beyond
the lake called Hussein Sagar in a house in Musheerabad,
hometown of my mother's family, I have locked
myself in a bedroom. My uncle has just explained to me
that what I have is not a mental disease after all
but a spiritual one, that the devil has entered
my heart and made me criminal. That I let him.
That I would not resist him is further proof
of moral deficiency. My aunt hovers in the kitchen
during the lecture, wringing her hands, hoping
it turns out for the best. When he is finished
she brings me a glass of warm milk and almond meal
flavored with saffron and rose-water. "Did you have
a nice talk?" she asks, her voice trembling a little bit.

They leave me there in the apartment, fashionably
furnished in a modernist style, offering to deadbolt
and padlock the door behind them for my safety and though
I refuse, I bolt myself into my room anyhow and stay up
all night. My uncle asked me how I, raised a Muslim,
could turn my back on a whole lifetime of teaching
while my cousin's wife Alicia, raised in rural Wisconsin
as a Christian somehow found her way to Islam. He kept telling
me in our conversation that Alicia was a "new Muslim" that she
could lead both Americans and Indians to what he called "truth"
because unlike many in my own generation of our family, he points out,
Alicia covers her hair, makes her daily prayers, found a way to follow.
But unlike most converts I know Alicia did not change her name.
Why should she? That name means "noble" or "truthful," depending
on who you ask. What is truth anyhow? Is the truth my body
tells itself enough for me to know it or must I be taught
out of some book written in a language I never knew.
All through the night I fastened myself to lonely stars
and the glowing screen in order to still the seismic
shock of Hyderabad. My body wasn't the only one that was
failing: I saw that same night the note from Alicia
that my cousin Shabbar had been diagnosed with
a dangerous cancer. On the surface of Hussein Sagar
night-birds scream. My body has never belonged in the world.
God and I were secret lovers hiding in the closet from my friends
and His. When He put his tongue in my mouth my body
came alive as a beast, an animal, the wild creatures
that roam the night of my imagination. It's true I learned
the religion of my parents not just by heart but by rote,
repeating verses, casting their vowels deep into my throat,
pasting the consonants to the roof of my mouth. Arabic
changed the muscles of my breath and made poetry possible.
How then did my favorite imam become not Imam Kazim
for whom I was named and at whose shrine a thousand people
died during Bush's War, when the bridge they were on collapsed,

but instead Imam Raza, the one who fled the Arab world, fled
into Persia to save himself and his sister, from the government
that sought to write him down criminal and pull his body
into the earth. He made for India, but delayed over-long
in the mountains of Qom where the snow casts its melody
in ivory dust like the flutter of bird's wings against paper
or the surgeon's light tool flickering through Shabbar's body.
It's a trick that history outside has nothing to do with history
inside. A trick that God's words as believed by heathen others
aren't also graven in fire in my own body. And though I turn in,
tune out, the stiletto of the world spikes through: a young gay man
in California has a bottle broken over his head. #MuslimBitch
#Trump2016 spray-painted on the side of a building. A cafeteria
full of schoolchildren begin chanting "Build the wall!" We're here.
It's now. A black man accused of selling cigarettes without a license
is strangled and killed. A group of white men who staged an armed
occupation of government property are acquitted. But stop. Those things
happened before. So what has changed and what hasn't? In Hyderabad
on a hot summer night, the electric fan groaning overhead I turned
all the lights off and read in the dark the screen in front of me
flickering with messages from Alicia. We held on to that tether
all night long, though ten-and-a-half hours apart it was me who
spent all night sleepless talking with Alicia about illness, about
recovery, about how bodies fail, about what prayer was really worth
and Alicia who gave up work for a day to lie on the couch, laptop
on her stomach writing to me about God, who He loves and
how no one gets to choose that or explain it. About what faith does
and doesn't mean, about who does their prayers and at what times
during the day and what form do they take. Today, a long
time after Hyderabad, a long time after I thought I would feel
safe forever and I did until I didn't, I try to find an armature
for grief, for loss, for the end of a certain kind of world. I crave
no light tether now. My commented-upon body in the library
that could be a highway is published in wilderness wanton.
Starving among the desert rocks, put upon, blogged about,

pissing away the silence, while far out to sea still unnoticed
a new nameless tropical depression gathers around an eye.
I remember one childhood summer when I was sent to stay
with my boy cousins to learn my proper model, proper games.
Amid those forms of hardness I discarded the text in favor
of the wind. Humble to start a nation a notion one galaxy wide
with its bureau of infernal propagation. Wild plants to betray
the soil. Our surface now roils with the unreal, wind through wheel,
does not god want to win and flout the unspoken? At Hussein Sagar
a sand crab crawls the lake's skimpy wrack line. Water meets earth
in the form of the broken. Body is where fire and air enter
among earth and water. A painting is the meeting of eye
and touch. Mind the river out of reach but heard through the trees,
felt on the skin. River is sculpture unfolding in time. Such a quick turn
then, unmoving, my body so cruelly useless. Bodies now being beaten
and killed, this tin emptiness now turned back and what is this rage.
I wanted to break everything in the house but my body wouldn't dare.
All these trees planted for future shade. That long-ago summer
the only games I agreed to play involved brightness and bird calls.
In Hyderabad in the night I reached out across the wires to any friend
while outside loomed the dark rocks which broke apart millions
of years ago and ended the reign of the dinosaurs on Earth. In the end,
my uncle never brought up our conversation again, just tried to be friendly
as if it never happened. Shabbar lived. And I started to see Alicia
was like me, an outrider. She chose a new faith but kept her own first name.
Her middle name she changed to "Naseem," meaning the morning breeze and
her last name is "Razvi" now. It means "from the family of Reza,"
you remember him? — Reza. The imam who wandered.

INQUISITION

Those who acted like Lisbon was a letter written

Directly to them I had to remind the Inquisition reached

All the way across the water to Goa and flayed bodies open

We are by violence this language given in every place a sun

Body can now so sweetly envelop itself in water

I am the boy underwater hoping somehow to breathe again

This pinup boy for sin who wants to devour but ought

To be himself devoured having had too many lives.

Forgetting to be reborn, I don my cape of blades to steal

Into the capital of Loneliness, no one there knowing whether

I am a believer or betrayer of sound and the language of water

I was not born into it but coaxed it from sky and seed

I usurped from the riverbank its inheritance

My gospel is still that night in the cold autumn in Portland

Having just learned of the assassination of Rabin

High on Thunderfuck we climbed up the fire ladder to the roof

Looked out over the wind-washed city, the cloistered ruins.

He was straight but we were alarmed in the world

And knew then of only one way to be alive.

He drew down his silk long johns and I took him in my mouth.

From him then I sipped sound, the moon, the flocks of nightbirds

Calling, I let the language of flesh fill me from lips

To throat and when the inquisitor flooded my mouth

I knew in thrilling despair that time is yet untestified,

Water so far in the life of a human untraveled and no answer

Would ever satisfy but Heaven is this Earth —

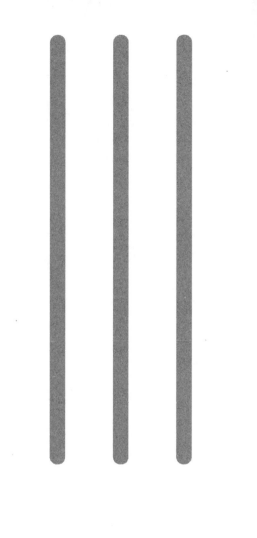

BIRD HOSPITAL

Hurtling down uncaught by updraft he receives the page
Saying cast off the woven coat of feathers and all the ice-
Sheathed vestments and scrub in

The doctor is the beast he was warned about who will try
To makc him whole and dizzy from his fall he can't protest
When his song turns monstrous

Nested in the anger he never wanted to be woven into this
Bird made of bull and swan thundering on so no wonder
The sutures fail in the traffic of wings

Now in the unraveling operation lonesome
Haunted by malpractice and terrifying winds
Abjuring the night's belated suit he solo wanton sings

MARIE'S CRISIS

We stumble through the strafing night to any harbor we think safe
and we find one on some corner in the West Village called Marie's Crisis
and in it scores of men huddle around a grand piano and sing songs
together. At some point, a woman who looks like Helen Terry,
the big backup singer from Culture Club, emerges from the kitchen
to sing a number for the boys.

The crowd falls silent and she starts belting it out and immediately
I want to know *wait what* is *the crisis?* And immediately after *why
is a song called a "number"?* I know Pythagoras believed that music
resonated between planets and that the notes of the scale could be
calculated, that each note itself was not even singular
but had a dominant tone with seventeen other harmonic tones underneath.

Or am I making all this up? And why do you care?
And why haven't you taken your pants off yet?
Marie is singing Janis Joplin and I imagine that I can actually feel
the porosity of the table under my fingers. There's a cute skinny blond
at the bar. He's wearing a short-sleeved plaid shirt which I think
I can get on board with but ironed jeans with boat shoes, not so much.

I'm trying to figure out exactly what to say to him but my field is
physics not chemistry. I open with "I wrote my dissertation
on the agitation that occurs in world-sheets during a redshift event."
Not my strongest effort. He responds with, "In Indian dance, the face
is actually an instrument of the body and so its expressions
are part of the choreography."

Marie looks like she's about to burst out laughing. I know the look,
it's called "show-tune face." Look ridiculously happy while belting out
whatever song at hand at the top of your lungs. No one cares, she's singing Sinatra.
I met a kid in Brooklyn once who said he was Frank's son: he grew up
with his mom in suburban Jersey and Frank never acknowledged him
but used to come around and have dinner with them every once in a while.

It was the night my friend Ava taught me how to take tequila shots
and I had seven and ended the night chatting up Danny
in between his stints dancing on the bar.
I found I didn't really have anything to say to him except
that I believed him, that I thought Frank really was his father,
that he looked just like him.

As soon as I'd said it "These Boots Are Made for Walking"
came on the radio and I thought it pretty likely that was a sign
but I didn't say anything and I don't know what Danny was thinking
because he didn't say anything either. Marie is singing a bluesy,
folksy version of "I Saw the Sign" and it makes me remember
my friend Araki who used to be my lover and then only my friend

but maybe isn't even that anymore because I haven't heard from him
in eight months and I have no idea what he is doing, because
all he ever posts on Facebook are links to news stories about public health.
Marie's voice is scratchy and smoky and whiskey-soaked.
It's not even what you'd call pretty or good but she is singing
for everything she's worth. The bar is cute but small and a little shabby,

and the blond wants to know if I'll sing a duet with him
when Marie is done and that makes me think either I better
marry him or make a run for it while I've still got some lead time.
I can't sing but I have developed an equation that can calculate exactly
how long it is going to take for you to take off your pants.
Don't say physics doesn't have any practical applications.

Then someone tells me that's not even Marie, it's Maggie the night manager.
It's been a week since that club in Florida got shot up and my parents still
haven't called. Maggie is singing the Boy George part of "Church of the Poison Mind"
and I'm three sheets to the wind anyhow so I'm going to climb up on top of that
    piano
and do the Helen Terry part. Maggie's voice is straining and it's not even
her crisis. She's the biggest star in the room, girl needs backup.

MISSAL

Sent to the placement office in unseasonable cold
I am a sealed letter, the salt of the sea weeping its agreement
to be stitched into form, clamoring for a shot at assuming
the chores of annotating the categories of sin.

Spiked by sun I am the noon's bright spittle,
the direct result of mid-spring snowstorm and lake effect,
my bones whittled into the shape of a man,
tending the tired plot of salvation history.

In the snow's loose register I log my disbelief abandoning
no fickle ally and strain to hear the chambers of time roar
their assent to my application for release from the rules of calumny,
drowning out shame's white dismissal.

Last year's forgotten seeds break the icy surface
and I swear myself to spring's sodden earth.
At the rain soaked rubble of the last stingy archive
I claim no satisfaction in victory. Eat dirt. Whore.

YANNIS RITSOS

Athens was welcoming to those who had come from the sea.
MAHMOUD DARWISH

Yannis, you held him in the glare of the diamonded sea,
unteaching him his practical mantra of liberation,
seeing in him a son to take care of you in your loneliness,
loneliness varnished by your detention

in the house made of flower stems that thrust
through the rocks in the prison-yard, its roof made
of the unscannable lines of rain. You revealed to him
the sound of the rusty-hinged door, how it would swing

sadly open and reveal no homeland beyond at all.
He came from the sea dragging his anklets of keys.
Did you teach him then how the old locks and houses
of his hometown were already all broken?

Yannis, in the end he rinsed the last of the coast road's
dust from his body after a lifetime of pressing his language
into lines of poetry and prayer and prestidigitation,
tired of praising mosques in which he could not pray.

The same morning I was forbidden by the guard to pray
at the Mosque of Cordoba, he woke up in Houston,
Texas and went to a mall food court to meet for the first and last time
his translator. The words they spoke to one another

were the same as those I saw in stone fragments
on the floor of the archeological dig at Madinat az-Zahra,
the ruined capital of the West looking East toward
the cities left behind. That city had remained buried

in a field for a thousand years. The palace and throne room
had been torn apart, the rubble of the mosaics
now being painstakingly reassembled piece by piece,
unlike the villages of Palestine, disassembled down to stone.

Yannis, what did you say to him that blue afternoon when the stone
canoe landed and he arrived in another place that would be home and
not-home? In Cordoba, meanwhile, the story of his death flashed
across the morning news, scrolling along the screen from clay to nothing.

But let's let the sea have the last word, the sea he crossed to come
to you, or the one that sparkled off the coast of Chile when he,
in Neruda's house, remembered you or the sea that rained
lightly down as the poet and his translator huddled together

over cheap mall coffee to converse, in Texas of all places,
though it could have been Athens, or Palestine, or Neruda's house,
at least as good as any mosque in the world,
so long as there was coffee and poetry and the sound of rain,

rain in the shape of the river, rain in the shape of a broken lock,
rain in the shape of long-since written verses, while the translator
of lost homelands makes from the sound of butterfly wings
rain in the shape of the dark furnace of days.

RANDOM SEARCH

Who will in the night unpetaling lose himself in fealty
His crime heartbreaking, confessed and festering
What undresses in the ground, lost in perjury

He's to be tried for the nearly unforgivable sins of naming
ordinary stars after himself, drinking coffee without labor laws
Marking time by the icicle melting from the eave

Chaste and chastened, he is touched by you
His body changes as he sinks under your hands
The world's opulent answer, his silent umbrage

A submerged body arrows to the surface
Not by intent but because it is buoyant
He wants to save you, wants to save everyone

Hand him back his glasses and he tells you to
Renounce meat and demand an end to inheritance
And then he's off to recite Arabic in the gate area

What else is left but to be human here

SQUARE

Caught between slaughter and capture
Hovering over the geometry of battle

Distance evergreen distill and claim me
I am changing to tiger or flame

In the wild lunar penumbra
I pitch a tent on the raft of the sea

Divine my hand this shame of sun
Like a chess piece on its square

that has only one move to make
I am led back to the combat zone

in which I was born
Gossiped about by god

Taut like a string that sings umbilical
Sought like a sailor drunk in the wind

SUN WARD

But the sun was shining, and some of the people in the world had been left alive, and it was doubtful whether the ridiculousness of man would ever completely succeed in destroying the world.
GWENDOLYN BROOKS, *Maude Martha*

And sew I sow the night   to the whore   I   son: are the son   but the sun

Re: chords   each sin   that since   was seen   was shy   was shining

There sun   to sum   and some that swan   each sing to son   and some

I soul   to sell   these cells that   foal   cos: sin: I quell and   of the people

Called   they killed   my self   a lie   ally   or lined   my cell   in the world

No matter   that hurt   I heard   what killed   a calc   ululation   had been left

Unheard   unaccounted for   in the ledge   for which   God's book   thrust lies   alive and it was

Then deader   that shelter   dreadful weather   and again   sounded out   and spied   doubtful whether

We could found   as unfound citizens   new loss   these laws   based upon   the ridiculousness of man

Sew I then   in wood   and thatch   natural swatch   and shook seed-pleats   would ever completely succeed

Stories vaulted

Loose and swore   sure sand   to shore   enlightening   unstoried   stored   in destroying the

Fault lines assaulted do lie   untoward   still on this sword   this sward   this sun-won   world

TEXT CLOUD ANTHOLOGY

Afternoon alive angel Ali
Belted by birds
Blue boat of your body
Breaks in breath
Broken brother come in
dark disappear down
Don't exist
The empty editor echoes
Eternal fast find me forgotten
The garden glass hasn't heard yet
To hollow its horizon higher
Inside Kazim
Kazim knew
Learned light
Listened
Lived lost
Limited himself to matter
His memoir of morning
Mother mountain mouth
Never night this orifice open
Orating to ovation
Plucked pot pieces of plot
His prayer pulled quickly from rain
Recitation of rain rejoining the rocks
Rocks rushed to remembering the secret series
Of sun wonders, silence on the shore
Silence someone sounds
Speaking through stone
The sunset stringing us along
Students of the task that of thirst

A thousand trees to teach this trick to us
To understand the voice the verse the version of vanishing
That waits and wants and wonders
Wheel window wander
Yesterday you yearned in the yews
You know then who you were
Who you gathered yourself to be
Zamindar of zinnias
Zephyr through the zoo

FORGOTTEN EQUATIONS

One (through the window I do charm

(My father (when I am a boy)

(In a place real not real)

(And spin a chrysalis of sun)

writes in light four pages

To claim god don't know)

+ One (and in delight

(Flying west in the last light)

My handloom kismet) explains

(Sad as a cinder))

(Does not) = (anything)

(I weep like a stone)

(Really close to) two

THE ASTRONOMER'S SON

At my birth, he whispered the equations of gravitational resonance into my ears and so taught me to calculate orbital positions of unseen objects.

I have learned these days to finally say without my voice trembling: *my father and I are separated from one another by a great distance.*

We had only the language of the heavens to explain ourselves.

When I was six, he used fishing twine to string up nine foam balls around the ceiling lamp in my bedroom, coloring each one with felt-tipped markers.

Like the moon I turned evenly around him, always keeping one part secret.

He drew me a map each night on blank chart paper. Taught me what I would see: *The Hunter. The Little Dog. The Lyre.*

Between the solid inner planets and the outer swirling intangible ones are the ruins that hold the whole system together.

And why did Saturn collect rings or Uranus lie on its side? And who can say why I grew into what I am?

Not the language of the heavens but the language of heaven that pulled us from each other. In an astronomical equation even one digit of difference introduces light years of error.

Sometimes in my loneliness I recite to myself what snatches I can remember of what I was taught: *In the shoulder of the Herdsman is Arcturus, the giant orange star.*

To live I will have to forget the math of round orbits, the rule of even planes. To be true to what I know about the universe: *14,000 years ago, the North Star was one of the strings of the Lyre. 12,000 years from now, it will be again.*

I hurl my doubt down into all the unfolding time it takes solar music to resound against the outer planets.

After all, *Of all the stars in boundless heaven, it's the Little Dog that shines the brightest.*

ALL ONE'S BLUE

In the empty rooms of sky I lingered
For a year and a day only now
Do I wonder in which blue vestment
Dawn will I don in thunder raiment
Rains and send this letter to far
Gods who knew nothing of how
A room by cloud and atom warm
Could add to a human body the share
That birds have to roam no room
Then clear to the horizon mark a vertical
Creature bear I earthbound and clever
Beyond measure do swear oblivion
Has its own markers but where the buoy
Of being clangs its stellar ore

DOOR BETWEEN YOU

In the cabin next door you hear voices

That keep you awake in the lumbering night

What slumber slackens will open in lack

The sleepless philosopher on the other side of the wall

Going on and on about how we are all creatures of energy and light

"Reachers" you could buy but what in hell are "injuries of light"

SON OF HISTORY

I ruin my work with love or oil

but unsoiled I return to the toil of stars

Stained by their light traveling

from the galaxy's edge,

I hover here now unspooling

knowing neither infinity nor dirt.

LEGISLATURE

Now I require like the formless legislature of clams a humble armature
That does not even need spin in odious threads a glamour of pearl

I am a poet lying in jail for leaving the scene of the crime
Themselves little pages, their pages unstunned his verses sung
His name not mud but music not the strings harmonic
but one that vibrates
My name same as him
who hurled the medals into the river
and went to jail on his own free will

What am I punch drunk demanding to be taken seriously as a man
When in the vault of the sealed Sayeeds I dreamed of a different life by the shore
Our darkness off the grid interrupted
By the revolving beacon of the lighthouse

Smuggling walrus bones in my suitcase I who stood once among the broken
tombstones of Birwe choose a new name for myself
one unpronounced unnoticed slowly over six hundred years

In both cases bound by what came before us now destroyed

Sent to wood or down into earth

You don't get to the end of it

Day breaks into us like the lighthouse pierced the deep southern sky

Buries us and breaks our graves

Hollow and hollow hardly a prayer

My voice sonorous lost in summer when the town empties out and I find myself full
of anger and sore my body sick and I get old and am forgotten

I write a book about my lonely self traveling across borders and checkpoints but to
find what

How strange to be in a body tired or sick or under duress

Pythagoras thought that the space between planets had a resonance that could be
translated as music which means what, that the sky could read us and not the other
way around

In the house made of string or woven branches the *eruv* I hide inside unable to sleep
We wait for the meteors to appear summer shower but they do not come
I alphabetize all morning hoping to experience the world in more than tatters

And the bodies of lovers uneven, braided together like a hermitage hut
Wounded we are in the net, not weak at all but immense confluences
And now I am emptied in the summer rain, running loose errands

House of silence, we have forgotten how to talk to each other
One poet who was born in a girl's shape but chose for himself to become a man
describes for me that moment as a young girl he put on a dress to go visit god

While in a town outside Columbus another poet writes in his notebook,
"we are a journal death is keeping"

I deny myself food because I want to know the body by its lack

I want in the coming year to take every fake quiz on the internet I can find
To learn which goddess I am
Which *Firefly* character I am
Which tarot card I am
Which planet
Which beat poet
Which desert bird

I want to set myself on fire in a rain storm
In this "long life of having-looked as a way of believing"
"you are making yourself punishable the flood said"

Now in the tea house called Sanctuary the man reads the verses inscribed on my
arms, debates its translation
He says "this does not say 'I am a Muslim. The rose is my *qibla*.'
It says: 'I am Muslim. God lives inside a rose.'"

Looking out of the small rectangle at the bright day, the people passing by and cars

I could be in any city at all, not here in my life.
At any moment, not in August, at a family wedding
to which I could not bring my lover.
Hiding in the darkened interior of a tea house called Sanctuary
told again about the shifting truth of
what I believed so strongly I wrote it into my skin.

A woman lights her cleansing herb
A man is sharing his pumpkin seeds
They talk about what changes in your perceptual abilities when you cut your hair

Legislature of enslaved fire draws all kinds of hasty conclusions
Passes sentences on poets who arduously unscrew meaning from image

Thorned down son drowns
Shorn the sun's sound
I am the son thrown down

Spoke noon sun mouth speak
Me always untorn and enslaved
Weird notions of gender and ground
Nothing but you between me and god

Share your seeds then
Veto every law
Say how well it turns out
When you choose your own body
When you choose the wrong card
When you deny what even all the stars in heaven had planned for you

APASMARA CLIMBS TO THE MOUNTAIN LAKE

First at the shore the water so blue it disappears into the afternoon of my eye
I am marked by flowers, my body a boat that seeks to cross the wide reach of it
Abandoned by those who accompanied me
My old fear of depths returns and I wonder
How long divided by valley and springfall will I be allowed to stay
Here, ungoverned but thrilled by light and salt I turn up the rock-trail to seek
The long-lauded gorge all the others were permitted to climb to long ago

As I hop the stile to follow, I look back
To the beach and see small figures moving
Was that how I too was seen? Having never thought to climb before
The matter feels not unimportant but irrelevant. After all, the shape
One's body makes in the ocean cannot be mapped
But here on the trail I hold close all my failures:
That I am always afraid of being unloved
That I am the stupidest person I know
That I do not call my mother
That I forgot my sunscreen

There's always in the back of my mind the blue blank of my old hometown,
Long since claimed back into the Canadian wilderness
And all the hometowns before and after that I never claimed, never found a home in.

The current of the world buffets us, we cannot be still, the deeper we go, the calmer
But I always stay here where the breath of the depths
Comes in and the undertow wants to drag me back out

The well of the deep *wants* us
The deep life — sex, god, death — it *wants* us

Land, like the body, has a shape that can be seen and known but what I know
About my own body is almost all wrong
It's a flowering plum that decorates my arm in bright pink, not a cherry like
everyone always tries to sell me on

Can I be entered
Can the ocean make me
Can the flower know me

I am already written down in gunfire and criminal code
The seeds of next year already in the ground, remember
The phenomenal sun unfurls
A million geological years shift the rocks of the trail up
Above the surface of the water
These rain patterns
These subvolcanic seismic shifts
These plants and birds yield to the history of an island forming anew

Neither map nor molecule I am battered
Fractal coastline extrapolated from patterns of moss on a tree
Or the electron's sonic path

Yes I know — "sonic" is wrong
I'm no scientist but I have a song
It vibrates neither in seven tones nor twelve but in all the space between
Usually thought of only as a whine or hum

Water tumbles now from the ridge into the icy mountain lake
Tumbles not without pattern but in fulfillment of Shiva's dance,
Entropy which is chaos of order unspeakable

I heard the painter of waterfalls once say she does not utilize craft or technique but
rather makes decisions and so perhaps god is a little bit like that

Low as a lawman, god chooses colors and canvases
And then the day like paint poured from the top and allowed to fall uncommanded

Beacon spree of bullets can light any dark

My mother's voice allowed through the pulse of world-noise

Still, supposedly the universe wields its laws
A body must fall
Water may not stay in the same state
Rain follows physics
Opera sonnets song box to the quantum point of et cetera

Lookit: Chance, Liquid and Gravity are hardly the type of gods a boy would put much
faith in but in my case those were the only ones who would accept me into their
worship

They said:
Light every candle
Cross your fingers
Stake your claim to being the dumbest thing that ever lived
Oh but wow I should be so lucky because unless I can release every line inked
How will the new ocean ever be able to enter and know me

I'm no beautiful thing
Most days I can hardly stand up straight and breathe
My whole time in the earth has ground down to this degradation:
That even this poor unloved body, these stark days
Even abandoned I seek height
Even while you are opening and entering me, killing me,
I am too much a brute to get the hint

Water screams down from the ridge into the gorge
Equations scatter in a spangle of flower light
Ground down into ignorance and death
My cheek against the sticky rock
God's foot between my shoulder blades
Pressing all the air out of me
My blood freezing in the shock of mountain pool
Burning in shame for not being able to muscle up and rise
Crushed by every element ever invented
Yet I will not relinquish this ignorant ugly shape
I rage I snarl
I want
This life

Gratitude to the editors of the following journals who published some of these poems in earlier and sometimes differing versions.

Academy of American Poets Poem-of-the-Day: "Letter to Hyacinth from the Once-Wind Zephyr" (as "Dear J."), "Drone"

Almost Island: "The Tornado"

American Poetry Review: Earlier version of "The Labors of Psyche" (as two separate poems, "Tower of Babel" and "Plunder"), "The Astronomer," "Atlas," "Chopping the Birch," "Yannis Ritsos," "Night: A Celan Variation," "Marie's Crisis," "Apasmara Climbs to the Mountain Lake"

Asian American Literary Review: "Amerika the Beautiful"

Bat City Review: "Missal," "May"

The Believer: "Trick"

College Mathematics Journal: "Forgotten Equations"

Congeries: "Abu Nuwas"

Cordite Poetry Review: "The Astronomer's Son"

Fact-Simile: "Door Between You"

Iowa Review: "Messy Drunk," "Saraswati Puja"

Kenyon Review: "All One's Blue," "Son of History," "Checkpoint"

Literary Hub: "Sun Ward"

Nat Brut: "System Error," "Screen Door"

Nepentla: "Bird Hospital"

New England Review: "Letter to Zephyr from the Once-Boy Hyacinth," "Origin Story"

New Republic: "Text Cloud Anthology"

Normal School: "Flower Gate"

Plume: "The Dress-Maker of Galilee," earlier version of "The Labors of Psyche"

Poem (UK): "Light House," "Missal"

Poetry: "The Earthquake Days," "The Failure of Navigation in the Valley"

Stanford Journal of Asian American Studies: "Sent Mail"

Starting Today: 100 Poems for Obama's First 100 Days, edited by Rachel Zucker and
    Arielle Greenberg (University of Iowa Press, 2010): "Random Search"
Tin House: "His Mosaic Prayer," "John," "Inquisition"
Viz.: "Phenomenal Survivals of Death in the Mountains"
Volt: "Legislature"
West Branch: "Persephone as a Boy"
Western Humanities Review: "Square"

In addition, "The Earthquake Days," "Screen Door," "Legislature," "Text Cloud
Anthology," "Flower Gate," "The Astronomer," "Abu Nuwas," "His Mosaic
Prayer," "Random Search," "Chopping the Birch," "All One's Blue," "Bird
Hospital," "Letter to Zephyr" and "Yannis Ritsos" appeared in earlier, and in
some cases significantly different versions, in a section entitled "Psychophonic"
in Kazim Ali, *All One's Blue: New and Selected Poems* (HarperCollins India, 2015).

A book is a constellation of cosmic events and a poem is too and a poet himself
too. It is impossible to think of all the people who helped me make these poems.
But some of them are: Zubair Ahmed, Kaveh Akbar, Rachel Tzvia Back, Stephen
Coger, Matthew Dickman, Maha El-Sheikh, Blas Falconer, Mary Garvin, Dana
Hamdan, Kamden Ishmael Hilliard, Genine Lentine, Layli Long Soldier, Shane
McCrae, Rajiv Mohabir, Stephen Motika, Ian Rhodewalt, Domenico Ruggerio,
Ralph Savarese, Emily Savarese, Sam Sax, Emily Siegel, Ramkrishna Sinha,
Sridala Swami, Jude Theriot, Marco Wilkinson, Irma Wilkinson, and Mark
Wunderlich.
    Special thanks to David Young, Jed Deppman, Caroline Jackson Smith, David
Walker, Lynn Powell, Jessica Grim, and Nancy Boutilier. As well to Jim Walsh,
Rachel Jagoda Lithgow, Matthew Hayden and Sean Safford.
    I had a turning point at the Lambda Literary Retreat — those fellows Emily,
Lauren, Mat, Sam, Kelly, Ife-Chudeni, Paul, Russ, Bryan, Imani, Sara, and Annah
gave me life.
    In particular, to the editors who have stuck with me, including Suzanna·
Tamminen, Elizabeth Scanlon, Alex Dimitrov, Karthika VK, Don Share, Rick
Barot, David Baker, and many others, I thank you.

"The Earthquake Days." Allen Ginsberg and Agha Shahid Ali enter into the poem
to try to shake some sense into me.

"Flower Gate." Since the venue appears to be Haifa, the speaker may be the boy
Anees, who demanded to share the fate of the Bab, founder of the Baha'i faith,
when he was condemned to face a firing squad.

"The Astronomer." Haifa was built on the side of Mount Karmel, site in ancient
times of observatories, in modern times the shrine of Bab. Astrology is not,
strictly speaking, illegal in Islam but there are many warnings about its use.

"Abu Nuwas." The pseudonym of a seventh-century half-Arab, half-Persian
poet who appears to have been as equally fond of God, wine, and handsome
youths. His sobriquet means "Father of the Locks" apparently referring to the
long tousled curls by which he was known.

"Light House." The three quotes are from the writings of Agnes Martin. The
phrase "lonely evangelist" is taken from Cammy Thomas's book *Cathedral of
Wish*. "Opon" is Emily Dickinson's particular, consistent spelling of the word
"upon."

"John." John Street in lower Manhattan abuts World Trade Center Plaza. I lived
on John Street for a brief time in the fall of 2000.

"Letter to Zephyr from the Once-Boy Hyacinth." In the myth, Zephyr the Spring
Wind and the god Apollo competed for the affections of Hyacinth, son of Clio,
the Muse of History.

"Labors of Psyche." When Psyche betrayed her vow and shone a lamp over the
features of Eros so she could see him, Eros was forced to abandon her. Psyche
competed a series of labors to earn back his love.

"Text Cloud Anthology." Created from the text cloud of "frequently appearing
words" that appeared on the website for an e-chapbook, *Pluck Me and Hum:
Selected Poems*, which was released in India.

"The Astronomer's Son." A sharp astronomer will notice that the son is
misremembering his father's lessons, including the critical one: Procyon, the

main star of the constellation Canis Minor, is in fact only the *seventh* brightest star in the sky.

"All One's Blue." The title is from a line in Agha Shahid Ali's poem "Barcelona Airport": "Behold how to hide / One must like God // Spend all one's blue."

"Legislature." In 1975 Muhammad Ali claimed that fifteen years earlier, heartsick at the racism he had met when returning to the States from the 1960 Olympics, he had thrown his gold medal into the Ohio River. Though many people believed Ali was exaggerating or telling a tall tale, the medal was recovered from the river (and donated back to the Ali family) in 2014. "Mohammad Kazim Ali Sayeed" is my full given name. Birwe was the home village of Mahmoud Darwish in the Galilee. It was one of the villages evacuated and destroyed by the Israeli military groups in 1948. The first quotation is from Barton Smock, the second and third are from Jorie Graham, and the fourth and fifth are from Sohrab Sepehri.

"Apasmara Climbs to the Mountain Lake." Apasmara in Hindu mythology is known as the dwarf of ignorance. Shiva dances the cosmic dance on his back, suppressing him. Apasmara is one of the only demons in Hindu mythology who is immortal; Shiva cannot kill him because without "ignorance" in the world there would be no "knowledge" to attain. Pat Stier is "the painter of waterfalls." I heard her lecture at the Allen Art Museum in Oberlin, Ohio.

KAZIM ALI is a poet, essayist, fiction writer and translator. *Sky Ward* (Wesleyan University Press) was the winner of the Ohioana Book Award in Poetry; *The Far Mosque* (Alice James) won the New England/New York Award.

In addition to editing *Jean Valentine: This-World Company* (University of Michigan Press, 2012) and *Mad Heart Be Brave: On the Poetry of Agha Shahid Ali* (University of Michigan Press, 2017), he is the founding editor of the small press Nightboat Books and the series co-editor (with Marilyn Hacker) for both the Poets on Poetry series and the Under Discussion series from the University of Michigan Press.

He has taught and lectured at colleges and universities across the country, including Oberlin College, Naropa University, and St. Mary's College of California.